HOW TO LEARN
FROM
A COURSE IN MIRACLES

Other Books by Tara Singh

How to Learn
from
A
COURSE
IN
MIRACLES

TARA SINGH

FOUNDATION FOR LIFE ACTION
Los Angeles

First limited edition, Foundation for Life Action,
February 17, 1983.
First edition, Coleman Publishing, 1983.
Revised edition, Foundation for Life Action,
October, 1985.

Library of Congress Cataloging in Publication Data

Singh, Tara, 1919-
How to learn from A course in miracles.
1. Foundation for Inner Peace. Course in Miracles.
2. Spiritual life. I. Title.
BP610.S56133S56 1985   299'.93   85-24790
ISBN 1-55531-000-1 Revised edition, hardbound
ISBN 1-55531-001-X Revised edition, softcover

The material from *A Course in Miracles* and *The Gifts of God* is used by permission of the copyright owner, the Foundation for Inner Peace, Tiburon, California.

I am most grateful for the goodness of the following friends for assisting in the preparation of the revised edition of this book: Lucille Frappier, Jim Cheatham, Aliana Scurlock, Clio Dixon, Sandra Lewis, Norah Ryan, Ted Ward, and Charles Johnson.

Contents

THE WILL OF GOD

There is a silence and a certainty
Apart from time; a peace and quietness
Surrounded by a thousand angels' wings,
And kept inviolate by God's Own Hand.
It is for everyone. Yet very few
Have found it. It will wait for everyone
Who seek, and all of them will find at last
This secret haven, hidden from the world,
And yet in open sight. Its clarity
Is blazing, yet it is not often seen.
Its call is constant, yet is rarely heard.
Attack must overlook it, yet to love
It gives an instant answer. Here the Will
Of God is recognized and cherished still.
And it is here that finally God's Son
Will understand his will and God's are one.

This poem is from *The Gifts of God* by the scribe of *A Course in Miracles.* It is an incomparable book of poetry containing some of the most important words ever spoken.

Foreword

As I emerged from a three year period in silent retreat, I was introduced to *A Course in Miracles* for the first time. For me, it was the meeting of the Spirit of *A Course in Miracles*. I recognized instantly that it was the Thoughts of God.

This contact with *A Course in Miracles* completed something in me. I knew my function the minute I read:

> *Nothing real can be threatened.*
> *Nothing unreal exists.*[1]

What took place in that instant has never left me. It is a bond with another Reality, the impeccability of which inspires one.

I had often wondered why, out of all the scriptures of the world, there was not a single step-by-step approach that a person could pursue unto application. I was very impressed by Moses parting the sea, and the wondrous things the other God-lit men and prophets had done, but it did not alter anything in me. It was not my light.

I rejoice that *A Course in Miracles* has its own day-by-day curriculum, as one is held by the hand and led to one's own eternal purity and holiness.

A Course in Miracles invokes the inherent memory of God that initiates an awakening within. It is for the active man living in the world and requires little time for its application. It emerged out of the New World to bring mankind to new consciousness.

The Course is an action. It does not condemn or judge anyone. It does not react to religions. It deals with the student who reads it, and takes away the idea of dependence and of following another. It brings the student to the discovery of potentials within himself that will enable him to impart something of eternal value.

Once you have the eternal to give, insecurity no longer arises and conflict ends. The question lies in changing. And to change — to be transformed — requires integrity and self-honesty. I have known two God-lit beings, and both have emphasized, ''People seldom ever change.''

The lessons of *A Course in Miracles* have to be brought into application. Nothing will work unless the truth of the Course is lived. Everything depends on the individual and his integrity.

To discover one's own God-given function is the great gift of Life. What is natural is effortless. The struggle lies in removing the distorted perception of who we assume we are. Being free from his own beliefs is what man calls difficult.

Man's function is to bring the Kingdom of God to earth. He is the bearer of Grace and his holiness is a blessing upon all that is.

Tara Singh

Introduction

What can I say about this book
that endeavors to represent the spirit of
A Course in Miracles?

The very benediction the Course imparts
silences me.
It is an action of the Grace of God.
Unhurried, read it lovingly.
The moment you are relaxed,
wisdom will surround you
and the Given becomes accessible.

A Course in Miracles is a joyous adventure.
Each lesson imparts its blessing all day long.
It awakens you to gratefulness
and to your God-given function.

Be still and listen to the truth.

> *Into Christ's Presence will we enter now,*
> *serenely unaware of everything*
> *except His shining face and perfect Love.*
> *The vision of His face will stay with you,*
> *but there will be an instant*
> *which transcends all vision,*
> *even this, the holiest.*
> *This you will never teach,*
> *for you attained it not through learning.*
> *Yet the vision speaks of your remembrance*
> *of what you knew that instant,*
> *and will surely know again.*[2]

Part I

How to Learn from A Course in Miracles

A Course in Miracles is a systematic, Divine order of education that reveals our innate perfection. It consists of three volumes: *Text*, *Workbook for Students*, and *Manual for Teachers*.* There are three hundred sixty-five lessons, one for each day of the year.

Reading the Course invokes within you energies that you may never have been sensitive to before. All your questions can get answered. Its purpose is to provide self-sufficiency and eliminate the false premise of helplessness. Therefore, it is to be lived and not just to be read.

> *Do you not see that all your misery comes from the strange belief that you are powerless?*[3]

We cannot apply *A Course in Miracles* as long as we are satisfied with ideas, because the Course is not an idea. It is not abstract. It does not talk about something. It speaks from the actuality of Truth Itself.

---

*The *Text* sets forth the concepts on which the thought system of the Course is based. The *Workbook for Students*, three hundred and sixty-five lessons, is designed to make possible the application of the concepts presented in the *Text*. The *Manual for Teachers* provides answers to some of the basic questions a student of the Course might ask and defines many of the terms used in the *Text*. (Editor)

If you have seen the limitations and the falseness of ideas, then you come to stillness, and you communicate with something beyond your own thought. This is the purpose of the Course, to bring ideas that cannot know love or truth to an end. Can we read it this way?

It is reverence that gives us the space to receive that which is not of thought, but of Grace. Reverence frees us from thought and brings the mind to stillness. It activates the heart. When you love something there is the reverence, for it becomes total and whole and has its own atmosphere. Therefore, it is important to learn to read with reverence and space.

A Course in Miracles comes to us at a time when mankind needs a scripture that teaches application. All scriptures are vertical words. Scripture is only scripture when it is not born of separation with God. The purpose of scripture is to end man's limitation and bring him to the wholeness that he is.

Learning according to *A Course in Miracles* is the miracle that undoes the belief system of separation. Thus, the basic issue we face is the separation in us that promotes fear, loneliness, and insecurity; and then, in turn, the wishes and wantings of unfulfillment.

Miracles offer us the clarity of inner awakening that is the direct experience of,

> *Nothing real can be threatened.*
> *Nothing unreal exists.* [4]

The miracle of the Holy Instant would bring you to objectivity and reveal this fact. It is a different kind of learning.

The ability to see the false as the false is to be free of the false. That moment of freedom is religious. It is the space where the miracle takes place. But if you do not put your whole attention to it, then you are stuck with an idea and not a miracle.

Man's thought system promotes the separation, no matter how sensitive and wise and good its ideas seem. Miracles undo it.

A miracle frees us from the past and future.

Clarity frees us from desires, suffering, and anxiety — for these are self-made, in ignorance of Reality.

Reality is the Will of God, the light of perfection. It is the Divine Decision. The wise, having seen the fallacy of personal decision, makes but one decision: to never make a decision independent of the Will of God.

In our unawareness we make decisions out of loneliness and uncertainty. But there are no uncertainties in Life, nor confusion where there is love. Only desires, ambitions, and want of activity lead to personal decisions. If we are grateful and at peace, then we discover all needs are already blessed and met.

REALITY IS THE ONLY DECISION.

Knowing this, we would not be slave to our misery that projects wishes and wantings. If we read with a still mind, we know with certainty God takes perfect care of us. This realized, there is no need for anxiety or worry. This is the Peace of God.

Man is meant to be at peace and in harmony with life, for AS IS is perfection. But the question is, do we really KNOW this? Are we at peace or are we children of insecurity?

We are talking about *A Course in Miracles* and how to learn from it directly.

Every day we read a lesson from the *Workbook*. For example,

> *Love created me like Itself.*[5]

We may think we know what the word "love" means, but do we? Honesty is required to know the truth of it.

As long as we are content with just words — and most of us are — we will never get to know what it really means. Why is it we have not questioned a word we use so frequently, to discover what is the actual state of Love?

Love, which is of Heaven, is the only state of being that is not pressured by time or anything external. Every single knowing is external to it. Every single word, including the word "love," is external to the actual state of Love. It is uncontaminated by words, and it renews itself every moment. Each of us is of the authenticity of Love.

Every second the planets rotate. What energy! Can you conceive of how many billions upon billions of breaths are taken every second? And all that breathes grows. Can you see the energy behind Life? That energy is what Love is; and the whole of creation is an extension of it. Its first impact dissolves all words, and brings one to innocence, to the purity of a saint. The state of being that knows the Real has the right to use the word "Love." Nothing else has.

The action of the Course is that of Love. It does not influence because it is an action of the awakening of Love, which is independent, and must therefore provide freedom and liberation. It restores your identity with your reality and eternity.

As long as we are going to keep using words without knowing the reality behind the words, we will not know what *A Course in Miracles* imparts. We need to give it space and read it with a quiet mind that is not pressured. Offer your stillness and it will be filled with peace.

How we approach learning from *A Course in Miracles,* and the quality of honesty we give it, is all important. We do not want to turn its teachings into another belief within the limited thought system of man, for *A Course in Miracles* is the Thoughts of God and awakens one out of thought to one's own boundlessness.

The *Workbook for Students* begins with the lesson,

> *Nothing I see in this room [on this street, from this window, in this place] means anything.*

It goes on to say,

> *Now look slowly around you. . . .*[6]

Have we paid any heed to the word "slowly"? Have we ever done so? Probably not. It is not all that easy to slow down the thought process. It is like saying "relax." Does your pulse come down instantly because you have used the word "relax"? But if you are in a reverent atmosphere, where you love what you are going to be reading or doing, you are already prepared. You have already stepped out of the momentum of tension and activity, and found a few moments just to BE. The action of relaxation is that it widens the gaps between the thoughts.

Then, when you read, *"Now look slowly around you,"* you have given yourself the freedom and space to do so.

There are constant reminders in the lessons of the Course that stress "unhurriedly," "slowly." These must be essential because the very first line of the first lesson states:

> *Now look slowly around you, and practice apply-*
> *ing this idea very specifically to whatever you see:*
>
> > *This table does not mean anything.*
> > *This chair does not mean anything.*[7]

The Course insists that you are not to make the practice ritualistic. Ritual means repetition of something. Just saying the words of the lesson does not mean anything.

Could you really look at the hand before you and say,

> *This hand does not mean anything.*

The Course begins with the undoing of our belief systems and our knowings — the bondage in which we are caught. It is our conclusions that are being questioned, and the question has the vitality not to accept any of our own verbal answers.

Undoing is essential because we are so highly conditioned. What we think we know is seldom real, for it is only our opinion. We stop short, conclude, and therefore, we never see the whole, the total.

Separated as we are, we tend to separate everything. Anything that is in isolation, to which you give a name, is unreal because everything is part of the whole. And unless we see the whole, we are not seeing at all.

Each lesson of the Course brings our separation to our awareness, and in an instant, an awakening to end that separation. For to know the truth is to bring it to application instantly.

> *The truth is true. Nothing else matters, nothing else is real, and everything beside it is not there. Let Me make the one distinction for you that you cannot make, but need to learn. Your faith in nothing is deceiving you. Offer your faith to Me, and I will place it gently in the holy place where it belongs. You will find no deception there, but only the simple truth. And you will love it because you will understand it.*[8]

Within that moment you can behold eternity. Therefore, you are free from time, and you discover your own reality, your boundlessness, its sacred moment. That is the moment in which the miracle has taken place. The miracle is when time ceases and eternity is.

The Course has much more to give than intellectual knowledge. It is to end the separation in one's life and bring one to the wholeness of one's being. One is cleansed with the purity of one's own Reality!

> *I am not a body. I am free.*
> *For I am still as God created me.*[9]

Where there is the body, there is thought. They are not two phenomena. If one came to the truth of *"I am not a body,"* then one would say, *"I am free."* Each individual would realize, *"I am still as God created me."* Concepts of punishment, karma and guilt, come to an end.

A Course in Miracles is based on each person's inherent perfection and our approach to reading it should be based on our perfection as well.

If the god we seek is a god born out of our unfulfillment, he will end up being a projection of our unfulfillment. A projection is an image, not the truth. The Course says,

> *God is with me. I live and move in Him.* [10]

True relationship exists at the eternal level. The river is related to the ocean, to the sky. Everything is related. Nothing can exist by itself. Relationship is that you are related to the planets, to the light, to the earth, to everything. You could not exist without them for nothing can exist in isolation. In relationship, there is no such thing as fear, insecurity, or unfulfillment.

The flower is a flower, and it is not unfulfilled. It is the joy of its own perfection. A flower has no wishes. It does not want to be a chair, or a pot. If you could see the flower, it could bring you to stillness. Your distractions and wishings and wantings would end also. For in that moment you are related to wholeness.

Look at the star and it introduces you to your own eternity. Light years away, but you can relate with it. If you have truly seen it, it silences your mind. If you are preoccupied while looking at it, you merely look but do not see.

The Course tells us,

Miracles are seen in light.[11]

This is not the physical light of the sun. The sun is a small affair. There are other spheres that are not lit with this little sun. This is a Light that has a million suns in it.

It is the Light in which there is understanding. It is not an understanding of something; because then, that thing is there, and you are here. Do you see the separation so-called understanding creates? To the Light of awareness, nothing is outside of you. We are talking about a state where appearances disappear and One Reality is.

Unfortunately, we have, over the centuries, become obsessed with the accumulation of more and more knowledge. This mania of moreness keeps unfulfillment alive and is what regulates our intellectual faculties. Can we approach learning from a new premise: fulfillment?

We are talking about learning with an intent to be free of preoccupation, and not to accumulate information. Thus, we read differently.

Jesus continually repeats in the Bible,

"He that hath ears to hear, let him hear."[12]

Will you listen? We usually do not listen because we interpret what we hear and read with our own thoughts. We are listening to our interpretations, are we not? We assess the other person: I like this; I do not like that. And the chatter goes on.

The minute we are really attentive, thoughts cease. For example, we are attentive if we run into a rattlesnake. We do not interpret whether it is male or female.

We are capable of coming to attention. But as long as we are lukewarm, we are not going to do so. We fall back into thought that says, "I am going to do it tomorrow." Thought lives by postponement.

We never see that postponement is a thought process, and it is not real. It is still ideas. It will crumble away because ideas, like emotions, subside, rise and fall. There is no consistency in them.

But there is consistency when we are totally attentive, because in that moment, we are free from brain activity. There is space to be part of the Mind of God that we are.

We will know the Mind of God when the chatter of the brain is silenced. The brain has its senses; it is used for survival; it collects memories. But the mind is the Mind of God of which we are all a part.

When the brain does not interfere, stillness introduces us to the Mind of God. We discover that every single being is blessed, being part of the Mind of God. And there is no longer any separation between you and me. At the brain level, there is separation. At the Mind level, we are all One.

It is the Mind of God that is religious, not the brain. The brain can be Hindu, Moslem, or Christian. It is conditioned, shaped by the environment, by personal experience. But the Mind of God is neither conditioned nor subject to experience.

Once that fact is established, our relationship with *A Course in Miracles* undergoes a change. We become more attentive and read it differently. We can read a lesson in the Course, which would be using words to begin with, but every sentence would lead us from our thought to the Mind of God.

This is the unique thing about the Course. Organized religions tell us what Jesus did, what Mohammed did, and what Lord Rama did. *A Course in Miracles* does not tell us what somebody else did. It does not preach. It brings us to stillness and to the Mind of God. This all depends, however, on how serious and with what quality of reverence we read it. If liberation is our interest, then we value there is something that has, inherent in it, a blessing to take us out of our thought process — our brain preoccupation — to a different state.

While we read, there is the questioning of our unrealized words and the discovery of our attachment to our thoughts — thus, an awakening to the newness beyond the words. This actuality of direct experience takes place in the reading of the Course if there is the attention.

My mind is preoccupied with past thoughts.[13]

This is the problem. We cannot harness the energy of the Present. We are not alive to the moment, to receive or radiate the creative energy of the Present that this planet needs. Man's function is to bring the Kingdom of God to earth. And most of us are lost in the past.

Lesson after lesson, the Course begins with questioning and undoing to free us from the past. It goes on to say,

I see nothing as it is now.[14]

What a simple way of saying it. The Course really is a course in miracles so that you come to truth, to wholeness, and to rightmindedness. It is in rightmindedness that miracles take place.

To say this sincerely,

My thoughts do not mean anything,[15]

is to save a lifetime. This is the tenth lesson. Is there anything in the world that can bring a person to this state and the innocence of humility within ten days?

As we read, we begin to value what the Course is, and the reverence and love for it increase. The lesson continues:

This idea applies to all the thoughts of which you are aware, or become aware in the practice periods. The reason the idea is applicable to all of them is that they are not your real thoughts.[16]

There are real thoughts of which we are not aware. This is quite a discovery!

We have made this distinction before, and will do so again. You have no basis for comparison as yet. When you do, you will have no doubt that what you once believed were your thoughts did not mean anything.[17]

What an awakening! It is like the Lord holding us by the hand, and in ten simple days, bringing a total transformation.

There is a great deal of joy and excitement in the Course. It brings one to passion. The interest is there, and we are getting closer to the Present and our own holiness. We are becoming our real Self.

The outgrowing is taking place. The newness is rearing its head. We are beginning to question our own fanaticism, the beliefs that we knew. Now we are willing to see — to die to the past and to conditioning. We are no longer subject to the past, and a rebirth takes place.

Then the significant eleventh lesson:

> *My meaningless thoughts are showing me a meaningless world.*[18]

To just see and serve the meaningless world and to die is to never have lived.

The Course continues,

> *A meaningless world engenders fear.*[19]

There is fear because our values are meaningless. One country holds one value, and another country holds another value. Because they are different, they clash; and both are meaningless.

But,

> *God did not create a meaningless world.*[20]

We see that there are two worlds: the God-created world, without which nothing would exist, and the manmade world of the meaningless. As we begin to free ourselves from the manmade world, we see that the God-created world is the sustainer. Man did not create the air we breathe, nor the water we drink, nor the night sky, nor the food we eat.

How we have cut ourselves off from the God-created world through anxieties and worries! So many of us spend our lives and God-given energy supporting the meaningless.

> *My thoughts are images that I have made.*

> *It is because the thoughts you think you think appear as images that you do not recognize them as nothing.*[21]

See that they are but your images.

> *You think you think them, and so you think you see them. This is how your "seeing" was made. This is the function you have given your body's eyes. It is not seeing. It is image-making. It takes the place of seeing, replacing vision with illusions.*[22]

The Course goes on to say,

> *These exercises will not reveal knowledge to you. But they will prepare the way to it.*[23]

The reader begins to see how he is caught in his own images. Vision is our natural state, and we have replaced it with the illusions of images. And the lesson comfortingly says that our images will be replaced. Inherent in every lesson, in every line, is the blessing to bring one to the clarity of truth.

It is the Will of God, His Power, His Blessing, that the

goal of the Course be accomplished within one year by anyone who studies it with integrity and devotion. Please realize what this statement means. What else could you ever want?

If there is the potential in any one lesson to bring you to wholeness, how will you approach it? Will you try to fit it into your scheme of life, your schedule? If so, you are not ready to fit into God's Mind. Are you willing to kindly observe this?

Are you reading *A Course in Miracles* as an idea, to improve yourself? The minute you reduce it to ideas, it is no different than anything else, and you have not received the miracle it has to offer. Why do we reduce it to ideas? Have we ever done anything else, whether it be the Bible, the Koran, or the Vedas? And what "I am" continues. Nothing interrupts the old. Somewhere we have to see that we have to outgrow the self.

We are talking about the approach because much depends on how we read. I have seldom met anyone who knows how to read. We read the words, but the words are not the thing. Our words have meaning at the level of unreality — things we have projected. Yet to dissolve thought takes a different kind of reading, a different quality of attention.

> *Forget not that the motivation for this course is the atttainment and the keeping of the state of peace. Given this state the mind is quiet, and the condition in which God is remembered is attained. . .*
>
> *To learn this course requires willingness to question every value that you hold. Not one can be kept hidden and obscure but it will jeopardize your learning. No belief is neutral.*[24]

Are you approaching *A Course in Miracles* because you really want to step out of the constant preoccupation that gives you no rest? Do you want to bring the deceptions of the brain to silence? If there is that burning need, then your relationship with the Course becomes different.

Yet people have read it over and over without realizing the truth of it. Can you read it with the intensity of interest that will bring you to the State? It requires that you place a challenge before yourself. For without seriousness, the reading becomes ritual. The brain loves habit; it functions in terms of routine.

Each sentence in the Course confronts us with a challenge. Can we give it the inner space to unfold? Usually when a challenge comes, we put it off. We do not recognize the cause of the inadequacy that cannot respond to the challenge at the moment.

Where does the energy go? How do we dissipate it? It is this questioning and awareness that brings about a change in lifestyle. In this urgency of response there is no gap, no time to acknowledge inadequacy. For helplessness is our belief. It is not a reality.

The action of helplessness is compromise. Are you willing to put compromises away instantly as you read? This is application. This is discovery.

We have to realize the importance of intent. Then there is urgency. Urgency brings one to attention. The vitality of urgency alone can deal with the nonchalant attitude of compromise, and in so doing, come to passion.

A transformation takes place. One becomes the co-creator. Do you read the Course as a co-creator, so that by the time you have finished, you have ended the compromise and you are totally present? It is such a different way of reading.

Whatever questions the manmade thought system is already the action of God's Grace. Right away the Course imparts to you a new willingness to see.

> *I am responsible for what I see.*
> *I choose the feelings I experience,*
> *and I decide upon the goal I would achieve.*
> *And everything that seems to happen to me*
> *I ask for, and receive as I have asked.*[25]

A Course in Miracles is a joyous adventure. It is not to be made into a habit. The daily lesson carries its blessing all day long. It becomes an effortless action, and a great joy.

> *My present happiness is all I see.*[26]

You need never be touched by the fear of insecurity, for it is largely psychological. Thus, you begin to extend the peace of God on earth,

> "Thy will be done in earth, as it is in heaven."[27]

And this is where you hold hands, as offered in,

> *If it helps you,*
> *think of me holding your hand*
> *and leading you.*
> *And I assure you*
> *this will be no idle fantasy.*[28]

What a benediction to know you have never been

alone! Light and Love — the Given — have always surrounded you. To realize that the Given is accessible is the strength.

What a gift of God to each one who has *A Course in Miracles*!

The Course helps us with the application of the truth imparted. Yet we know this intellectually, like we know that we should not lie, or we should love our neighbor. But we do not know how to bring it into application. The knowing of ideas does not mean much.

The idea is abstract because it is based on duality. The Course does not go into duality. It dissolves the duality even between you and God. It says your will is one with God's. And God's Will is your will.

Gradually, we are getting used to the One rather than to fragmentation and separation. What a miracle! You would think one would leap with joy for discovering one is and can be liberated.

The Course states we have become conditioned and are caught in habit and error. It points out that these can be corrected.

> *Truth will correct all errors in my mind.*[29]

Correction is your function. Having met your function, you become an extension of the Course. And because errors can be corrected, you cannot be indifferent to your own or anyone else's.

When your function becomes

> *Salvation is my only function here,*[30]

conflict ends and you realize,

> *I will accept my part in God's plan for salvation.*[31]

By now, you must learn to extend what you have realized as the truth. When you begin to extend, then you become the bearer of Light. Thus the Course brings you to your function.

> *For what God gives can only be good.*[32]

Can you trust in that?

> *And I accept but what He gives*
> *as what belongs to me.*[33]

Look at the honor God gives His Children. Having given us all creation, He then says, "You are not even under my obligation. This belongs to you." We are given freedom from the very beginning. What sacredness is the glory of God, our Father! There is nothing for us to want or be distracted by.

The *Workbook for Students* states,

> *All things are lessons God would have me learn.*
>
> *A lesson is a miracle which God offers to me,*
> *in place of thoughts I made that hurt me.*[34]

No matter what they are and how good they may seem, all the thoughts we make invariably hurt us.

> *What I learn of Him becomes the way I am set free.*[35]

What I learn from Him is the miracle, being a moment of clarity in which time ceases. What I learn of Him frees me from my own limited decisions.

*And so I choose to learn His lessons
and forget my own.*[36]

Can you forget your own? We are under the pressure of our needs, our tomorrows, our yesterdays, and the whole personality issue. At the miracle level, however, there are no personalities. You are in the present, and nothing else is real.

The Course shares,

I place the future in the Hands of God.[37]

What a carefree contentment!

It also says,

*The past is gone; the future is not yet.
Now am I freed from both.*[38]

How spacious is the eternal <u>now</u>. The Course is immediate. Can you feel instantly that you are freed from past and future? Will you no longer dwell on the past? The future is not yet, and so you need not worry about that.

If you are just going to read it, and not touch upon the state, then know you are depriving yourself. For as long as there is past and future, there can be no peace. Where past and future no longer exist, there neither is a body. Thought itself disappears. If the thought remains, then you have not read it.

I am sustained by the Love of God.[39]

You do not even have to seek it. You merely have to realize that Love is what you came to give. The choice is yours, having free will.

Father, it is today that I am free,
because my will is Yours. [40]

The choice is either peace, or thought of past and future, peopled with the personalities of unreality. You want the Peace of God, but it cannot be without letting go of the illusion of past and future ordeals.

An unlived truth remains untrue. To know the truth is to bring it to application instantly. In the absence of application, life remains personal.

To the Christ State, body and thoughts are external, for they are of the world of separation. Thought only came into being after separation took place, whereas salvation is the release from thoughts that hurt us.

The language of the co-creator is non-personal, thus different.

> *Is it a loss to find a world instead where losing is impossible; where love endures forever, hate cannot exist and vengeance has no meaning? Is it loss to find all things you really want, and know they have no ending and they will remain exactly as you want them throughout time? Yet even they will be exchanged at last for what we cannot speak of, for you go from there to where words fail entirely, into a silence where the language is unspoken and yet surely understood.*

> *Communication, unambiguous and plain as day, remains unlimited for all eternity. And God Himself speaks to His Son, as His Son speaks to Him. Their language has no words, for what They say cannot be symbolized. Their knowledge is direct and wholly shared and wholly one. How*

far away from this are you who stay bound to this world. And yet how near are you, when you exchange it for the world you want.

Now is the last step certain; now you stand an instant's space away from timelessness. [41]

The words of *A Course in Miracles* inspire you to the state of stillness. The Course carries its eternal peace and awakens the Light in you.

When you have read three-fourths of the *Text* and the *Workbook* then it says: You have come a long way, and now you cannot go back. Is that not beautiful? Something has happened to fundamentally change your life. Is that not a benediction?

The introduction of reason into the ego's thought system is the beginning of its undoing, for reason and the ego are contradictory. Nor is it possible for them to coexist in your awareness. For reason's goal is to make plain, and therefore obvious. You can see reason. [42]

When you come to the place where the branch in the road is quite apparent, you cannot go ahead. You must go either one way or the other. . . No one who reaches this far can make the wrong decision, although he can delay. And there is no part of the journey that seems more hopeless and futile than standing where the road branches, and not deciding on which way to go.

It is but the first few steps along the right way that seem hard, for you have chosen, although you still may think you can go back and make the other choice. This is not so. A choice made with

the power of Heaven to uphold it cannot be un-
done. Your way is decided. There will be nothing
you will not be told, if you acknowledge this.[43]

You have one more step to take. The Course says you
have the choice of going ahead, but you do not have
the choice of going back.

Then it states,

This course is easy just because it makes no
compromise. Yet is seems difficult to those who
still believe that compromise is possible.[44]

If you took the step, you would sense a new blessing,
a charge of vitality — a vivid sense of His Presence.

You have come far along the way of truth; too far
to falter now. Just one step more, and every
vestige of the fear of God will melt away in love.[45]

The only response you have is to realize you and your
brother are the extension of One Life. You no longer
look upon what he does in a body, but see his
holiness.

You would oppose this course because it teaches
you you are alike. You have no purpose that is not
the same, and none your Father does not share
with you. For your relationship has been made
clean of special goals. And would you now defeat
the goal of holiness that Heaven gave it?[46]

Choose, then, his body or his holiness as what
you want to see, and which you choose is yours to
look upon. Yet will you choose in countless situa-
tions, and through time that seems to have no

end, until the truth be your decision. For eternity is not regained by still one more denial of Christ in him. And where is your salvation, if he is but a body? Where is your peace but in his holiness? And where is God Himself but in that part of Him He set forever in your brother's holiness, that you might see the truth about yourself, set forth at last in terms you recognized and understood?

Your brother's holiness is sacrament and benediction unto you. His errors cannot withhold God's blessing from himself, nor you who see him truly. His mistakes can cause delay, which it is given you to take from him, that both may end a journey that has never begun, and needs no end. What never was is not a part of you. Yet you will think it is, until you realize that it is not a part of him who stands beside you. He is the mirror of yourself, wherein you see the judgment you have laid on both of you. The Christ in you beholds his holiness. [47]

This is the ending of the world — the illusion of appearance. Here one realizes the truth and value of,

"Love ye one another." [48]

And there is peace upon the earth.

Wherever there is such an awakened being, there is a radiance, a peace. Even the birds and the animals are not afraid, for it takes all the hysteria and the tensions out of the air.

And when such a being walks through the woods or through the city, he leaves that peace there. Everything becomes consecrated and blessed, for that being remains untouched by words.

Please do not underestimate yourself.

You carry a blessing with you.

Be at peace,
and know you are part of Eternity.

> *The certain are perfectly calm,*
> *because they are not in doubt.*
> *They do not raise questions,*
> *because nothing questionable enters their minds.*
> *This holds them in perfect serenity,*
> *because this is what they share,*
> *knowing what they are.* [49]

Part II

The Lesson of the Day

We would like to share with you Lesson 243 of *A Course in Miracles*. It reads:

Today I will judge nothing that occurs.

What would it take to overcome judgment? Can you imagine what a mind it must be that does not judge? What energy must it have?

NON-JUDGMENT IS OF A SILENT MIND.

The lesson begins:

I will be honest with myself today.

What would it take to bring this into application? Where would you and I begin? Merely reading it is not the truth. Mankind today is caught in the mania of learning. What good is learning if it does not bring honesty?

The lesson continues,

I will not think that I already know
what must remain beyond my present grasp.

What beautiful peace there is in this! It recalls humility with just the letting go of the words, without any agitation because,

Today I will judge nothing that occurs.

I will not think I understand the whole from bits
of my perception, which are all that I can see.
Today I recognize that this is so.

Recognizing is different from learning, or even the
pretentious word "knowing." To recognize means
that it is already there in you. But because we are so
busy with our little knowings, we never have the
space, the Holy Instant of which we are a part, a moment to recognize that I AM ONE WITH GOD AND
MY BROTHER, in truth. To recognize is to become
aware of a state of non-separation.

The minute you recognize, you are out of time, for you
have come in touch with your own boundlessness.
What a gift! Once you recognize your own holiness, so
will you recognize the holiness of another, for there is
no "other." This ending of separation is religious.

And so I am relieved of judgments that I cannot
make.

What peace this would be! How many millions of
thoughts are based on judgments? It is no wonder the
Course starts off with the undoing of all that is verbal
with which we are indoctrinated.

That would be silence. And silence would know
honesty, for it is free of deceptions. It is a purity. Of
this, each person is capable. You are as holy as the
prophets of the world.

Thus do I free myself and what I look upon, to be
in peace as God created us.

If one heeded these six lines of the Course, one would
be transformed. It does not talk about someone else,

or about Krishna's cosmic consciousness. It talks about you and who you are as God created you.

The lesson then concludes with a prayer. Having read a different lesson each day for two hundred and forty-two days, one should have come to the truth of this, having outgrown so much:

> *"Father, today I leave creation free to be itself. I honor all its parts, in which I am included. We are one because each part contains Your memory, and truth must shine in all of us as one."*

How meaningless are our words now.
How trivial our personal life with its preoccupations.
Inherent in the lesson of the Course
is the vibration and vitality to bring us to the Truth.

Of itself, the Course will give you perfection.
This is its service.

Conclusion

How one relates with the daily lesson of the Course is of utmost importance. Unless one's own energy is blended with intensity of interest, one will be able to give neither reverence nor the quiet space within. Mere reading will not realize the truth of the Thoughts of God the lesson contains. We insist that the Course is to be lived, not theorized.

The serious student of *A Course in Miracles* no longer lives by assumptions — he values what is Eternal, and for this, wholeheartedness is required.

Will you bring deceptions to an end in your life? Is not the undoing of deceptions the first function of responsibility? We cannot justify our being taken over by the externals without imposing or validating the weaknesses within us. Yet weaknesses are not real.

This realization is the breakthrough the earnest student of *A Course in Miracles* has to make to be an extension of the Mind of God. It is mandatory that the student go past learning to make it his own conviction. Only then will he know his own holiness.

References

1. *A Course in Miracles* (ACIM), *Text* (I), Introduction.
2. ACIM, *Workbook for Students* (II), Lesson 157, page 290.
3. ACIM, I, page 430.
4. ACIM, I, Introduction.
5. ACIM, II, Lesson 67, page 112.
6. ACIM, II, page 3.
7. Ibid.
8. ACIM, I, page 253.
9. ACIM, II, Review VI, page 376.
10. ACIM, II, page 392.
11. ACIM, II, Lesson 91, page 154.
12. Bible, Matthew 11:15.
13. ACIM, II, Lesson 8, page 13.
14. ACIM, II, Lesson 9, page 15.
15. ACIM, II, Lesson 10, page 16.
16. Ibid.
17. Ibid.
18. ACIM, II, Lesson 11, page 18.
19. ACIM, II, Lesson 13, page 21.
20. ACIM, II, Lesson 14, page 23.
21. ACIM, II, Lesson 15, page 25.
22. Ibid.
23. Ibid.
24. ACIM, I, page 464.
25. ACIM, I, page 418.
26. ACIM, Lesson 290, page 432.
27. Bible, Matthew 6:10.
28. ACIM, II, page 119.
29. ACIM, II, Lesson 107, page 189.
30. ACIM, II, Lesson 99, page 174.
31. ACIM, II, Lesson 98, page 172.
32. ACIM, II, page 384.
33. Ibid.

34. ACIM, II, Lesson 213, page 384.
35. Ibid.
36. Ibid .
37. ACIM, II, Lesson 214, page 384.
38. Ibid.
39. ACIM, II, Lesson 50, page 79.
40. ACIM, II, page 395.
41. ACIM, II, page 229.
42. ACIM, I, page 442.
43. ACIM, I, page 444.
44. ACIM, I, pages 460-461.
45. ACIM, I, page 468.
46. ACIM, I, page 466.
47. ACIM, I, pages 476-477.
48. Bible, John 13:34.
49. ACIM, I, page 109.

Biography of Tara Singh

Tara Singh is known as a teacher, author, poet, and humanitarian. The early years of his life were spent in a small village in Punjab, India. From this sheltered environment his family then traveled and lived in Europe and Central America. At twenty-two, his search for Truth led him to the Himalayas where he lived for four years as an ascetic. During this period he outgrew conventional religion. He discovered that a mind conditioned by religious or secular beliefs is always limited.

In his next phase of growth he responded to the poverty of India through participation in that country's postwar industrialization and international affairs. He became a close friend not only of Prime Minister Nehru and Mahatma Gandhi but also of Eleanor Roosevelt.

It was in the 1950's, as he outgrew his involvement with political and economic systems, that Mr. Singh was inspired by his association with Mr. J. Krishnamurti and the teacher of the Dalai Lama. He discovered that mankind's problems cannot be solved externally. Subsequently, he became more and more removed from worldly affairs and devoted several years of his life to the study and practice of yoga. The discipline imparted through yoga helped make possible a three year period of silent retreat in Carmel, California, in the early 1970's.

As he emerged from the years of silence in 1976, he came into contact with *A Course in Miracles*. Its impact on him was profound. He recognized its unique contribution as a scripture and saw it as the answer to man's urgent need for direct contact with Truth. There followed a close relationship with its scribe. The Course has been the focal point of his life ever since.

Mr. Singh's love of the Course has inspired him to share it in workshops and retreats throughout the United States. He recognizes and presents the Course as Thoughts of God and correlates it with the great spiritual teachings and religions of the world.

From Easter 1983 to Easter 1984, Mr. Singh conducted the One Year Non-Commercialized Retreat: A Serious Study of *A Course in Miracles*. It was an unprecedented, in-depth exploration of the Course. No tuition was charged.

Mr. Singh continues to work closely with serious students under the sponsorship of the Foundation for Life Action, a school for bringing *A Course in Miracles* into application and for training teachers of *A Course in Miracles*. He is the author of numerous books and has been featured on many videotapes in which he discusses the action of bringing one's life into order, freeing oneself from past conditioning, and living the principles of the Course.

Other Materials Related to
A Course in Miracles

Tara Singh

BOOKS

Gratefulness
"Love Holds No Grievances" — The Ending of Attack
How to Raise a Child of God
The Voice That Precedes Thought
A Course in Miracles—A Gift for All Mankind
The Future of Mankind (forthcoming)

VIDEO CASSETTE TAPES

A Call to Wisdom
A Call to Wisdom: Exploring A Course in Miracles
A Call to Wisdom: Wisdom in America
The Call to Wisdom: A Discussion on
    A Course in Miracles (Parts I & II)
Exploring A Course in Miracles:
    Scripture of the Age
Man's Struggle for Freedom from the Past
Moneymaking is Inconsistent with Life Forces
How to Read the Daily Lesson of A Course in Miracles
Life for Life
"Quest Four"
    with Damien Simpson and Stacie Hunt
"Odyssey" and *"At One With"*
    with Keith Berwick

37

AUDIO CASSETTE TAPES

A Course in Miracles Explorations, Series One:
Origin, Purpose and Application
Tara Singh Tapes of the One Year Non-Commercialized
Retreat: A Serious Study of A Course in Miracles

Additional copies of *How to Learn from A Course in Miracles* may be obtained by sending a check, Mastercard or Visa number and expiration date to:

FOUNDATION FOR LIFE ACTION
902 S. Burnside Avenue
Los Angeles, CA 90036
213/933-5591
Toll Free 1/800/732-5489
(Calif.)1/800/367-2246

| Limited edition, hardbound | $8.95 |
| Softcover | $4.50 |

Prices include postage and handling. California residents please add 6½% sales tax.

Thank you.